FIONA DOYLE

Fiona completed the John Burgess Playwriting Course in 2012.
Her plays include *Coolatully* (Finborough Theatre; winner of
the 2014 Papatango New Writing Prize); *So Gay* (winner of the
2013 Play for the Nation's Youth) and *Abigail* (shortlisted for
the 2014 Eamon Keane Full-Length Play Award). Her short
plays include *Rootbound* and *Rigor Mortis* (Arcola Theatre) and
Two Sisters (Southwark Playhouse). *Deluge* was the winner of
the 2014 Eamon Keane Full-Length Play Award.

Other Titles in this Series

Fiona Doyle

DELUGE

NICK HERN BOOKS

London

www.nickhernbooks.co.uk

A Nick Hern Book

Deluge first published in Great Britain in 2015 as a paperback original by Nick Hern Books Limited, The Glasshouse, 49a Goldhawk Road, London W12 8QP

Cover image: www.istockphoto.com/BalazsKovacs

Designed and typeset by Nick Hern Books, London
Printed in the UK by Mimeo Ltd, Huntingdon, Cambridgeshire PE29 6XX

A CIP catalogue record for this book is available from the British Library

ISBN 978 1 84842 484 5

Deluge was first performed at Hampstead Theatre Downstairs, London, on 16 April 2015. The cast was as follows:

KITTY	Elaine Cassidy
FLAN	Gary Lilburn
JOE	Edward MacLiam
INTERVIEWER	Charlotte Randle
Director	Anna Ledwich
Designer	Moi Tran
Lighting	Elliot Griggs
Sound	James Frewer

Acknowledgements

With huge thanks to Will Mortimer, Edward Hall, Greg Ripley-Duggan, Philippa Sutcliffe and all at Hampstead Theatre; Anna Ledwich, Moi Tran, James Frewer and Elliot Griggs; Camilla Young and John Burgess; Neil Flynn and Catriona Fallon; Billy Roche, Eilish Wren and the family of Eamon Keane; Nick Hern and all the team; Peggy Ramsay Foundation; Tom Hopkins, Amy Conroy, Judith Ryan, Declan Mills, Elaine Cassidy, Edward MacLiam, Gary Lilburn and Charlotte Randle.

And a very special thank you to Jocelyn Abbey for her faith in this play.

For John Burgess and Tom Hopkins

Characters

JOE, *early forties*
KITTY, *late thirties*
FLAN, *late sixties*
INTERVIEWER, *late thirties*
BARMAN
VOICE

Note on Text

Set somewhere in rural Ireland. Time period is ambiguous.

The actor playing Joe also doubles as Barman.

In Scene Eight, the man Kitty speaks to is unseen. We only hear a voice.

The song Kitty hums in Scene Eighteen should be the same one she hums in Scene Three and Scene Seven.

The card game played in Scene Thirteen is Rummy.

The sound in this play, like the sound of rain or the dogs barking outside somewhere, is particularly important.

A forward slash (/) marks the point where the immediately following dialogue or action interrupts.

This text went to press before the end of rehearsals and so may differ slightly from the play as performed.

Scene One

*Day three. Darkness. We hear rain. Lights fade up to reveal a
drab interview room. There is one small window positioned
high up.* KITTY *is waiting. A lock turns and the door opens.*
INTERVIEWER *enters and sits. Her hair is a little wet and she
carries a small red umbrella which she places on the ground
near the table. Door is closed and locked behind her by an
unseen person. As she speaks, she pulls a notepad, pen and little
Dictaphone from her briefcase.*

INTERVIEWER. Sorry I'm late. Hold-up at inspection. Well,
not a… 'hold-up' in that sense. (*Laughs.*) Someone didn't
have their ID. (*Pulls a deep voice.*) 'No ID, no entry.'
Pointless trying to… then there was a problem with the
second set of electronic doors so…

She smiles at KITTY *who remains expressionless.*

Pause. INTERVIEWER *ties back her wet hair.*

Raining again. Weatherman says it'll be on and off for the
rest of the week. Can't catch a break can we. (*Pause.*) How
are you? (*Pause.*) You seem calmer today. (*Pause.*) Did you
sleep last night? Warden says you don't sleep. But… sure we
have to sleep. We'd die otherwise. (*Pause.*) I'll keep coming.
Can't get out of it see. It's my job.

Silence. INTERVIEWER *starts arranging her items on the
table.*

KITTY. How old are you?

INTERVIEWER. Thirty-four. (*Beat.*) I lie. Thirty-six. (*Beat.*)
Okay, thirty-seven.

KITTY. You've lines on your forehead.

INTERVIEWER. Christ. Don't hold back. But it's good to
finally hear your voice.

Pause.

KITTY. I've lines now too. Joe used say I look like Maureen O'Hara. First thing he ever said to me. 'You look like Maureen O'Hara, like out've *The Quiet Man.*'

INTERVIEWER. Not seen it.

Pause.

KITTY. The sheets make me itch. I've a rash. (*Pulls down the neck of her T-shirt.*)

INTERVIEWER. Must be allergic to something.

KITTY. They use bleach.

INTERVIEWER. Right.

KITTY. Causes cancer. Pollutes the rivers and kills the animals. Not like it's news.

INTERVIEWER. I'll have a word with them. See what I can do. (*Makes a note.*)

KITTY. Sounds bad out there. Fields'll be waterlogged again. Cows'll have to stay in. There's so much to do. I need to get back.

INTERVIEWER. It's being taken care of.

KITTY. I need to get / back.

INTERVIEWER. It's being taken care of.

INTERVIEWER *makes another note.*

KITTY. Can I see him?

INTERVIEWER. Not possible.

KITTY. I just want to see him. Just for a minute or two.

INTERVIEWER. They won't let you.

Pause.

KITTY. Why are you here?

INTERVIEWER. Same reason I was here yesterday. And the day before that.

INTERVIEWER *places Dictaphone in the centre of the table and presses play.*

Day three. (*Looks at wristwatch.*) 11.30 a.m. Bad weather with risk of more flooding. But I'm not here to talk about the weather.

She looks at KITTY *for a moment. Sudden darkness.*

Scene Two

JOE *is working in a hay shed, stacking some hay bales and sacks of feed. There is a large object covered in sheets in one part of the hay shed.* KITTY *enters with a mug of tea. She watches him for a while. A dog starts barking outside somewhere.*

KITTY (*calling out*). Whist now would ya.

Dog keeps barking.

Be quiet!

Barking stops.

Fox I'd say. Saw one the last day. Out in the yard. Just stood there lookin' at me calm as you like. (*Pause.*) Joe. Please. You need to eat somethin'. (*Pause.*) Ya shouldn't be doin' that now.

She goes to him. We hear the sound of a bird shrieking. Dog starts barking again.

Whist would ya!

Barking stops. JOE *sips some tea.*

What happened yer hands?

JOE. The rope. When we was… lowerin' him in. (*Pause.*) D'you remember what he used say? 'Bout that? 'Bout buryin' him? 'Under the oak tree'll do me grand. Under the oak tree down the back field so's I can keep an eye on you all. Stand me up in the ground and turn me towards the enemies.'

KITTY. Ah stop, Joe.

JOE. Way they used bury the warriors. In the old times. Used do it that way then.

KITTY. Well we're not livin' in old times.

JOE. No.

KITTY. An' he wasn't no warrior. He was a farmer.

JOE. We're livin' in strange times now.

KITTY. I'm goin' in. Please, Joe. We only buried him today.

JOE. I'll be in in a bit.

KITTY. You said that two hour ago.

JOE strokes her face gently. He kisses her.

'Who gave you leave to be kissin' me.'

JOE. Don't make 'em like that any more hah? John Wayne. Maureen O'Hara. (*Studies her face.*) The spit of Maureen O'Hara. Like out of *The Quiet Man*.

KITTY. Even now?

JOE. Even now (*Kisses her gently on the forehead. Looks at her for another moment, then goes back to work.*) No. Don't make 'em like that any more. Shower of uncivilised cunts now. Immoral pack've bastards.

KITTY. Joe...

JOE. I'll be in when I'm in.

Dog starts barking again.

KITTY. Damn dog.

Exits. We hear her hushing the dog as she goes. Her footsteps fade away. JOE works in silence for a while. A clattering sound comes from the yard outside.

JOE. Who's there?

Noise again.

I said who's there?

FLAN (*calling from outside*). 'Tis me, Joe.

JOE. Flan?

FLAN. 'Tis only me. I seem to… have got me leg stuck in somethin'… (*Clattering sound as he frees his leg.*)

JOE (*to himself*). Feckin' eejit.

FLAN (*entering, drunker than he looks*). Joe m'boy! Sorry 'bout that. A bucket it was. (*Trips, but manages to keep upright.*)

JOE. Sit down there before ya kill yerself.

FLAN. A bucket with a hole in the bottom. Sure there's no use at all for a bucket with a hole in the bottom. (*Sitting and pulling out a flask of whiskey.*) I'm sorry fer yer loss, Joe boy.

JOE *sits beside him and takes a swig.* FLAN *takes his boot off and rubs his foot.*

He were a great man so he was. A great man an' he'll be sorely missed. He will now so he will. They're all still down there, Joe. All down O'Flaherty's raisin' a glass. Raisin' a glass to yer father.

JOE *hands the flask back.*

Silence.

Smell that damp, hah? (*Takes a deep breath.*) In the air that is. In the lungs. Jesus will we ever be rid. They say the mosquitoes are here to stay. They like the damp. Vicious little things so they are. The Africans has thicker skin see. Don't give 'em a second glance in the jungles over there. But us? We're not like them Africans. Sure what chance does the likes of us have against those wild little feckers all the way from the jungle in Africa? Killed a man up north they did. Newry I think. Killed him stone dead. Reacted bad to the bite they say. Feckin' malaria fer all we know. (*Puts his boot back on.*) Dark times, Joe boy. Dark times. (*Looks at the covered object stored in one corner.*) How's she doin'?

JOE. Halfway there.

FLAN. She's big enough isn't she?

JOE *shrugs.*

D'you hear about the Ark?

JOE. Hah?

FLAN. They think they might've found the Ark. The real deal like. Up a mountain somewhere. (*Whispers conspiratorially.*) In Turkey.

JOE. Turkey is it?

FLAN. Turkey! Sure aren't they all a bunch've savages over in Turkey.

JOE. We're savages everywhere. (*Pause.*) 'Nother storm on the way.

FLAN. The windows of heaven open up once again.

JOE. We'll have to keep the cows in.

FLAN. You're the boss. You're the boss now, Joe.

JOE. Go on away home, Flan. See you in the morning.

FLAN. Right you are. (*Stands. Considers something for a moment, then sits back down.*) I forgot.

JOE. What?

FLAN. The thing I had to tell ya.

JOE. What thing?

FLAN. Now I don't want to be... but I need to tell ya. 'Cause this is your farm now and you've a right to know 'bout things that be happenin' on yer own farm.

JOE. What're you on about?

FLAN. I wasn't sure should I tell ya see, the day that's in it an' all but...

JOE. Spit it out, Flan.

FLAN. Right. Right. I was down the back field this mornin' sortin' the cows out before the funeral like. An' I look up an' isn't there a rainbow in the sky. Drawn all across, from the sea out to the west. Lovely sight after all this cursed rain. Did you know God put the rainbow in the sky after makin' the deal with Noah?

JOE. No.

FLAN. Oh he did, Joe boy. He put the rainbow in the sky to seal the deal like. He'd send no more floods from then on. No more.

JOE. Well he's a fuckin' liar then isn't he.

FLAN. So anyways, I'm watchin' this rainbow an' thinkin' to myself, maybe there's an end to all this cursed rain after all, maybe our break's finally come, when I feels a set of eyes on me, boring into the back've me brain. So I turns round 'cause... well 'cause I can't help it an' that's when I... that's when...

JOE. That's when what?!

FLAN. I don't know, Joe! Fer the life've me I... a shadowy thing, corner of me eye but it struck me see 'cause it's like the way yer father said he used... an' then I look back up fer a second to see the rainbow disappearing an' the grey clouds come rushin' in, an' when I turns round again...

Pause.

JOE. Whiskey in the orange juice this mornin'?

FLAN. 'Twas exactly like what yer father / used say he –

JOE. My father's dead from the drink and the stress. My father... wasn't in his right mind from it all and well you know. Well you know, Flan.

FLAN. Aye. (*Looks up towards one of the beams in the hay shed.*) Aye, but he knew that beam would hold.

JOE. Go on home now. Been a long day. Go on home an' sleep it off.

FLAN. Joe, I'm just / tryin' –

JOE. I said go on home.

FLAN. But, Joe boy, maybe he weren't just imaginin' / things after all.

JOE. Get out, Flan.

Pause.

FLAN. Right. Right you are. (*Goes to exit.*) 'Tis a dark day. All gone mad so it has. (*Stops at door.*) I'm truly sorry fer yer loss. Aye, I am. See you in the light of day, Joe boy.

He exits. JOE *listens as the footsteps die away. Silence. He looks up at the beam.*

Scene Three

Day four. Darkness. A voice is humming gently, very sweetly. Lights fade up slowly and we see KITTY *standing with her back to the* INTERVIEWER, *looking out the window.*

INTERVIEWER *is fiddling with the Dictaphone.*

INTERVIEWER. You've a nice voice.

KITTY *stops humming.*

What's it called?

KITTY. I don't know.

INTERVIEWER (*speaking into Dictaphone*). Day four. (*Looks at wristwatch.*) 12.05 p.m. Should've started at twelve but couldn't get this damn thing to work. (*Places Dictaphone in centre of table.*) What do you see out there?

KITTY. Birds. Starlings. Painting pictures in the sky. Like they're… trying to tell us somethin'. (*Sits down.*) We know when the cows start gettin' agitated.

INTERVIEWER. Know what?

KITTY. That the rain's comin' again. The storms and the floods. Start beltin' their sides with their tails. Animals have better senses than us. (*Pause.*) They've started again, haven't they.

INTERVIEWER. East coast is hardest hit.

KITTY. I hear someone died. Trapped in a car.

INTERVIEWER. Did they?

KITTY. A woman I heard. She couldn't get out.

INTERVIEWER. That's awful.

KITTY. Did you know her?

INTERVIEWER. What?

KITTY. Did you know the woman what died?

INTERVIEWER. No.

Pause. KITTY *looks at* INTERVIEWER*'s notebook.*

KITTY. Who's goin' to read that?

INTERVIEWER. They will.

KITTY. Will they listen to the tape too?

INTERVIEWER. Can if they want. But it's for me mostly. So I can remember things.

KITTY. Some things are best forgotten. (*Pause.*) Did they want us to control the weather? Is that what they wanted?

INTERVIEWER. Where is he.

Silence.

Where is he.

Silence.

Do the right thing and tell me where he is.

KITTY. The right thing?

INTERVIEWER. Yes.

KITTY. The right thing.

She starts laughing. Lights fade. We can hear the rain in the darkness.

Scene Four

A weather report forecasting more bad weather with the likelihood of severe flooding comes from a radio. Lights up on KITTY *in the farmhouse preparing lunch.* JOE *enters.*

He's wet. Takes off his boots and overcoat. KITTY *turns off the radio mid-forecast.*

JOE. Waterlogged again. Cows'll have to stay in rest've the day. Washin' away parts of the road even. Fuckin' awful road that is now.

KITTY. They've it worse in other parts. We're the lucky ones.

JOE. Hear 'bout that fella up the country?

KITTY. What fella?

JOE. The one who died from the mosquito bite? Malaria they think. Flan told me.

KITTY. Flan once told me he saw the Virgin Mary standin' outside O'Flaherty's pub.

JOE. Who'd've thought hah? Malaria. Here. State've the place. Should be strung up the lot've 'em. Country's run into the ground.

She brings a plate of food over to him.

No money fer anything. Worse than last year. Get nothin' dried in this. An' government advice won't feed animals.

Phone rings.

JOE *goes to phone, picks up receiver and puts it back down almost immediately.*

KITTY. Who was it?

JOE. Wrong number.

KITTY. Didn't even give them a / chance to –

JOE. It was a wrong number.

He sits back down.

KITTY. What is it?

Pause.

JOE. Someone broke into Ned Callaghan's place last night. Emptied the feed store.

KITTY. What?

JOE. When he went down an' tried to… one've 'em had a gun. Bullet caught him in the face.

KITTY. Jesus Christ.

JOE. Flan's gone up to the hospital. He'll be a while. Back roads must be two-foot deep by now. They say he'll lose the eye. (*Pause.*) Folk are gettin' scared, Kitty. They're losing their animals. I know we've planned but… never thought it would get this bad. Fodder's running out. No money left. Animals need food an' food costs money an' all the time this rain, this persistent fuckin' rain. There's no end to it.

KITTY. It'll stop.

JOE. Will it?

Pause.

KITTY. Yer lunch'll go cold.

JOE. 'S all passing, Kitty. We're all just… stumblin' through. Like the sea pullin' in and pullin' out an' one day it might just wash us all away. Feels like someone's drilling a fuckin' hole in my head.

Silence. The rain is easing. KITTY *sits down opposite* JOE.

KITTY. I'm pregnant.

JOE. What?

KITTY. You heard.

JOE (*stares at her for a moment*). We're goin' to have a baby?

KITTY. I can feel it in me.

JOE. But they said… the doctors said…

KITTY. They were wrong. Sometimes they're wrong. But I'm scared, Joe. The world's gone all strange.

JOE. The world's always been strange.

KITTY. I don't know if…

JOE. Don't know what. (*Pause.*) Don't know what?

KITTY. If it's the right thing.

JOE. The right thing?

KITTY. Maybe it's not the right thing.

Silence. The rain has stopped.

JOE. Hear that? It's stopped.

KITTY. I'm… scared.

JOE. There's no need to be scared.

KITTY. I mean I'm scared for it. Not for me. For it.

Pause.

JOE (*placing his hand on her belly*). That's our baby. Our baby. All this time we've waited. Hah? Someone up there's lookin' out for us. He's up there now lookin' out for us.

The phone rings again. JOE *goes to answer it.*

Hello?

Scene Five

Day five. Raining heavily outside. INTERVIEWER *is on her own, waiting. She snacks occasionally from a little bag of nuts. After a while, she picks up the Dictaphone and speaks into it.*

INTERVIEWER. Day five. (*Looks at wristwatch.*) 11 a.m. Waiting.

She places the Dictaphone in the centre of the table. Eats a nut. Waits some more. Rain outside seems to get heavier. She speaks into Dictaphone again.

Weather: atrocious.

The door is unlocked and KITTY *enters. Door is closed and locked by someone outside.*

KITTY. Those toilets are disgusting. (*Sits.*) Have you noticed how dark it is? There's no light any more. It's just... dark all the time.

INTERVIEWER. It's winter. Gets dark earlier in winter. Nut?

Pause. INTERVIEWER *puts bag of nuts away.*

KITTY. Do you like stories?

INTERVIEWER. Depends on the story. I like funny stories. And I was obsessed with Dr Seuss as a kid.

(*Recites the tongue-twister about Fred feeding Fritz from* Oh Say Can You Say? *by Dr Seuss. Pause.*) It's from *Say Can You Say?* By Dr Seuss?

Pause.

KITTY. My mother used tell me a story as a child. About a saint, can't remember his name now. A saint who said the end would come with the arrival of a huge flood. The whole island would be washed away. She'd think of him every time it rained. I had nightmares about it. The same one all the time. Trapped in a small room with a locked door. And the water rising outside, spilling in through the window. A little window, very high up. I was always cowering in the same corner, watching the water come through the window.

INTERVIEWER. Maybe you should try some Dr Seuss. (*Pause.*) There are rumours, Kitty.

KITTY. Of course there are. Folk love the bit've gossip. They need it. It's a distraction from their own mess, isn't it?

INTERVIEWER. Please. Can you help them. Can you help them... start somewhere. Can you help them with that?

KITTY. Like they helped us? (*Pause.*) Joe's father used hear things. At night mostly. Said he saw things too. Shadows. Figures standin' in the field. We used think it was the drink. Flan found him swingin' on the end of a rope. No one came to help us. (*Pause.*) Poor old man. A good soul. Used give away the feed. They knew he couldn't say no. So they'd come askin'. The animals were starvin' an' they needed feed so he'd give it to 'em. All the surplus stuff. He was too... couldn't say no. Not when his neighbours' animals were starvin'.

INTERVIEWER. You must know somethin', Kitty. You must know where he is.

KITTY. I want him left alone. I want you all to leave us alone.

Silence.

INTERVIEWER *looks back through some notes.*

INTERVIEWER. The phone calls. When did they start?

KITTY. After Joe's father died.

INTERVIEWER. How often would you get them?

KITTY. Once a week in the beginning. Twice a day towards the end.

INTERVIEWER *makes a new note.*

Then they started... appearing.

INTERVIEWER. Who did?

A flood siren suddenly starts up. Shrill, loud. Very similar to an air-raid siren.

Who did?

KITTY *looks away.* INTERVIEWER *stops Dictaphone.*

Flood siren. Just a drill. Wait here.

KITTY. Like I have a choice.

INTERVIEWER. Warden'll be along in a minute. It's just a drill.

INTERVIEWER *exits. Flood siren is piercingly loud.*

Scene Six

FLAN *and* JOE *are standing by the large object in the hay shed, which is now uncovered. We see the wooden frame of a boat taking shape.* JOE *is measuring part of the frame.*

FLAN. Shame ya can't just buy one.

JOE. I've no money to buy one.

FLAN. It's a tall order if ya ask me.

JOE. Can read can't I? Got the plans right here.

JOE *takes a look at the plans while* FLAN *takes a closer look at the materials.*

FLAN. What kinda wood is it?

JOE. Pine. Knot-free. An' the grain is straight so it holds the nails well. (*Starts hammering.*) How was he?

FLAN. How d'you think? Sure he's blind in one eye the poor bastard.

JOE. No chance at all of savin' it?

FLAN. No chance.

JOE. Did he recognise any of 'em?

FLAN. Balaclavas.

JOE. Christ.

FLAN. 'And the earth was corrupt before God.' (*Slaps his arm hard suddenly.*) Little feckers! They're everywhere! (*Takes a look around, then speaks in a low voice.*) You know who I think done it? Broke into Ned's place? Those gypos up the road, that's what I think. 'Cause I hear they're selling feed in town. Fer a price that'd make yer eyes pop out've yer skull. Awful carry-on so it is. But the farmers are buyin'. Those what can.

JOE. What about those what can't.

FLAN. Eh?

JOE. The ones who can't buy the feed. Where they gettin' it?

Pause.

FLAN. Neighbour stealin' off neighbour? Ah no. No, no that's an awful accusation.

JOE. All gone pure mad though isn't it. Unprecedented times.

FLAN. Well I don't believe it. I don't.

JOE. All I know is I know nothin'. I know nothin' no more. (*Continues working.*) He was in debt. Lots of it. He hid it all. Hid it all till it got too much. No goddam life insurance neither. Can't bring meself to tell her. With the baby an' all. (*Pause.*) They've started callin'. They want their money. (*Hammering again.*) All that machinery he bought three year back? The loan he gave Ned Callaghan? The expensive feed from England? Couldn't afford none of it. An' lied to my face when he said he could. Givin' away feed right left and centre. Damn fool. Hold that end up higher. (*His mobile rings.*) Hello?… Speaking… How'd you get this…? I know that, I just… I said I know that, but… D'you think we control the weather do ya? (*Hangs up abruptly. Pause. His mobile rings again. He switches it off and starts hammering again.*)

FLAN. Shouldn't be doin' that now. Like drivin' a car when yer angry.

JOE catches his finger on the hammer, drops it, clutches his finger but doesn't make a sound. Then starts violently kicking the side of the boat.

JOE. They're all to fuckin' blame! The whole bloody lot've
'em! Shower of fuckin' muppets runnin' the place!

FLAN stands back and waits until he's finished.

FLAN. Sit down there.

They sit. FLAN *takes a flask of whiskey from his inside
pocket.*

In the words of Mark Twain, 'too much of anything is bad.
But too much whiskey is barely enough.'

They drink.

You'll have to tell her. Can't be keepin' secrets like that, Joe
boy.

JOE. I know.

FLAN. Sooner the / better.

JOE. I know.

Silence.

Someone tried to break the lock.

FLAN. Hah?

JOE. Our lock. To the feed shed. Last night. Dogs were makin'
a racket so I went down to the yard an'... I couldn't see
nothin' but I heard 'em. I heard 'em runnin'. Two, three
maybe. Things are startin' to go bad.

FLAN. Feckin' gypsies I'm tellin' ya!

JOE. Don't know who it was. Could've bin anyone. It was dark.

FLAN. Well it's wrong. Whoever it is. 'Thou shalt not steal.'
(*Pause.*) Or maybe... maybe it's them. Lookin' fer their
money. Tryin' to scare folk.

It starts raining outside.

Feckin' miserable weather. (*Pause.*) How long'll that take?

JOE. How long'll what take?

FLAN. To build her.

JOE. Couple've months maybe.

FLAN *takes another swig while* JOE *starts hammering again.*

Best keep an eye out now, Flan, y'know?

FLAN. Eyes like a hawk, me, Joe boy. Eyes like a hawk.

JOE. Good man.

FLAN *goes to the door and scans the yard outside. Lights fade. The sound of hammering rings out in the darkness.*

Scene Seven

Lights up on INTERVIEWER *on her own. She's lost in thought. She picks up the Dictaphone, starts rewinding, then presses play…*

INTERVIEWER'S VOICE. How do you feel when I read that?

Pause on recording.

How do you feel?

Pause on recording.

Shall I read it again?

Silence on recording.

'Two eyes looked up at me. At first I thought it was a dog. Sounded like a dog.'

Silence on recording.

'Moved like one. It was dirty. Its hair was matted.'

Silence on recording.

'The fingernails were / too long.'

KITTY'S VOICE. Stop it.

INTERVIEWER'S VOICE. Stop what?

KITTY'S VOICE. Yer twisting it.

INTERVIEWER'S VOICE. That's an eye-witness account.

KITTY'S VOICE. I had no choice.

> **INTERVIEWER** *stops Dictaphone and thinks for a moment. She then forwards the Dictaphone and presses play again. We hear the sound of* **KITTY** *humming.*

INTERVIEWER'S VOICE. Kitty?

> *Pause on recording.*

> Kitty?

> **KITTY** *stops humming.*

> What's wrong?

KITTY'S VOICE. I…

INTERVIEWER'S VOICE. What is it?

KITTY'S VOICE. Digging. I heard digging.

INTERVIEWER'S VOICE. Outside?

KITTY'S VOICE. In here.

> *Pause on recording.*

> Full moon last night. You see it?

INTERVIEWER'S VOICE. No.

KITTY'S VOICE. Watched it for hours. Full moon the night I met Joe an' all. He told me they're all in a line when that happens. The earth the moon and the sun. All in a line. Did ya know the moon's spinnin' away from us? Spinnin' away from us it is. An' if it spins out too far we'll all fall out of the universe.

> **INTERVIEWER** *stops Dictaphone and thinks for a moment. Then presses record and speaks.*

> **INTERVIEWER** *slowly recites the first two lines of the tongue-twister from* Oh Say Can You Say? *by Dr Seuss again. Pause. Then recites the last two lines very quickly. Pause. Then she rewinds and erases.*

Scene Eight

Dim lights up on KITTY. *She's facing the audience but it's difficult to make her out. Elevator-esque music can be heard coming from somewhere and it runs throughout the scene. She's clutching her bag and waiting for someone. Voices outside. Laughter. Door opens and closes quickly. Someone takes a seat opposite* KITTY. *We can't see them.*

VOICE. Sorry for the wait.

KITTY. That's fine.

VOICE. One of those days.

KITTY. It's fine.

VOICE. No end to it, hah? (*Laughs.*) Now. Wait just a moment.

We hear the tapping of fingers at a computer.

Just pulling up your file... there we go.

KITTY. I'd like to talk.

VOICE. Mmhmmm?

KITTY. It was for the farm. But / we've –

VOICE. Just a moment, just let me... Right. I see.

KITTY. I know it's...

VOICE. It is.

KITTY. I know that. But... my father-in-law and... and I'm pregnant as well but we weren't expecting it 'cause... and the weather, the weather, see? Same as last year. And the year before that. We lost some of the herd. And we keep havin' to buy it in y'see? The feed. You know that. So I want to talk to someone 'cause... 'cause we need more time.

KITTY *studies the face for reaction.*

My husband. He's tired all the time. Can't sleep, y'know? (*Pause.*) I mean, we just need more time.

VOICE. More time.

KITTY. More time.

VOICE (*sighs*). Just a moment.

We hear the tapping on the keyboard again.

I'm sorry. We can't. No room for movement here. I'm sorry but I don't make the rules.

KITTY. Then who does? (*Pause.*) So... what do I... how do I...

VOICE. Sorry.

KITTY. Stop saying that. Stop fuckin' saying that! (*Pause.*) He thinks he sees things now too.

Pause. Sound of typing.

What are you doing.

VOICE. Just... making a note on your file.

Silence except for elevator-esque music.

Scene Nine

Lights up on farmhouse kitchen. There's a rifle leaning against the wall in one corner. Sudden hammering at the door. Dogs are barking furiously outside.

KITTY (*offstage*). Hang on!

Hammering continues.

Christ's sake, it's open!

FLAN *lets himself in. He's out of breath.*

FLAN (*calling out to her*). Kitty! Kitty! He's gone after 'em! We saw the birds fly up out've the hedges an' the cows were all skittish!

KITTY (*entering; we see that she's heavily pregnant*). Gone after who?

FLAN. Them.

KITTY. Who's 'them'!?

FLAN. The shadows! Surroundin' the place. Lookin' in at us.
    All of 'em lookin' / in at us –

KITTY. Are you drunk?

FLAN. I'm not drunk!

KITTY. You'd better not be.

FLAN. We seen 'em! Just like… 'cept they're everywhere now.
    They're like the feckin' mosquitoes.

    KITTY *starts putting on her coat.*

KITTY. Comin' in here talkin' 'bout shadows and things
    surrounding the farm an' me eight months pregnant. If I find
    out ye've bin drinkin' I swear / to God I'll –

FLAN. I've not touched a drop. (*Beat.*) Apart from a quick swig
    at lunchtime but that was only fer to warm the bones.

KITTY. Probably a bunch of kids.

FLAN. I don't know, I don't know what's goin' on any more.

KITTY (*picks up a rifle and goes to exit*). Well? You comin' or
    not? (*Exits.*)

FLAN. Where you goin' with that thing? (*Follows her.*) Kitty?
    Kitty? Where you goin' with that thing?

    Dogs barking. We hear KITTY*'s voice hushing them. Then
    silence.*

Scene Ten

O'Flaherty's Bar. INTERVIEWER *is sitting at bar reading a paper by candlelight.*

INTERVIEWER. This is nice. Atmospheric. Olde worlde.

BARMAN. I wish.

Pause.

INTERVIEWER. When'll you get it back?

BARMAN. Sorry?

INTERVIEWER. The light.

BARMAN. Three hours ago.

INTERVIEWER. Suppose they're a bit snowed under.

BARMAN. Aye. Could be worse.

INTERVIEWER. You're on high ground at least.

BARMAN. Aye.

Silence.

Tough day?

INTERVIEWER. Sorry?

BARMAN. Don't look the type that drinks on a weekday.

INTERVIEWER. I'm loosening up.

BARMAN. Right.

Silence.

You're dealing with the case aren't you? (*Pause.*) How's the kiddie? Is it true what they say? Does he really bark like one? (*Pause.*) Can't talk about it? (*Pause.*) Whole world's gone mad if you ask me. Goddam weather. This one man got sucked into a drainage pipe.

INTERVIEWER. What?

BARMAN. With his dog.

INTERVIEWER. Jesus.

BARMAN. Oh yeah, US somewhere. Found them two streets down. What a way to go. Cars stranded all over the place, buildings collapsing. Mad. Least it's not that bad here I s'pose, hah? (*Pause.*) Another?

INTERVIEWER. No. Thank you. Best get off.

BARMAN. I knew the old man well. He was a good man. Just went a bit mad from it all, poor bastard. In the end, he was telling all sorts've stories. Dark shadows skulking round the farm. Strange sounds in the yard at night. Some say it was the stress. But others believed him outright. He owed a lot of money didn't he? An' they'll never give up on their money. It's all about the money. (*Pause.*) He'd get awful upset over his animals. Hard to watch your animals suffer. I remember him crying into his pint one night over two cows lying dead up in the field. Couldn't even move them to the knacker's yard 'cause the water was too high. Hated to think of the pain they went through. A kind old man so he was. An' now poor Joe gone missing… Awful tragic, the whole thing.

INTERVIEWER. Yeah. It is. (*Pause.*) On second thoughts, I think I will have another.

BARMAN. Right you are. (*Pause.*) D'you know, there's something… never mind. I'll get that drink.

Scene Eleven

Lights up. FLAN, KITTY *and* JOE *are sitting at the kitchen table.*

FLAN. That weren't no fox did that. A fox don't know how to use a knife. Unless it be a magic fox. An' I never seen that kind round here. Clean cut right across the throat.

JOE. Are ya sure ya didn't see it.

KITTY. D'you want me to lie, Joe?

FLAN. Weren't no fox did that.

JOE. It ran out from the hedge clear as day.

KITTY. All I saw was a pheasant. A pheasant fly up and away. Scared from all the noise we was makin'.

JOE. It ran out same time.

KITTY. An' the light was dimming.

JOE. Pheasant went up an' that thing went back. It went back across the field and into the ditch. How could you not see it.

KITTY. I seen nothin', Joe! 'Cept the birds an' the dogs an' the cows all huddled in one corner away from that dead one. Even Flan's admittin' he didn't actually see nothin'.

FLAN. I did not.

KITTY. You said it on the way back! How that when you think on it, it was more somethin' out the corner of yer eye.

FLAN. I felt somethin' then.

KITTY. You felt somethin'.

JOE. I saw somethin' / an' I'm tellin' ya –

KITTY. You saw shadows!

    KITTY *looks like she's in discomfort.*

JOE. What? What is it?

KITTY. Nothin'.

JOE. You sure?

KITTY. Yeah. Just… stop gettin' so worked up, will ya? Both've ya?

Pause.

JOE. Maybe it was to feed a family. Sure half the town's been washed away. Maybe we disturbed them.

FLAN. But to cut its throat like that? Why didn't they just steal her off first?

KITTY *winces.*

JOE. Kitty?

KITTY. I'm tired now. I'm tired from it all. Goin' fer a lie-down. (*Struggles to get up from the table, then collapses to the floor.*)

JOE. Kitty?! Can ya hear me? Get up! Get up, Kitty! Get up!

Sudden darkness.

Scene Twelve

Lights up on hay shed. It's early morning and FLAN*'s just come back from a lock-in down the pub. He is standing in the hay shed swaying slightly and humming to himself.*

He stops humming as if he's heard something, or sensed something. He looks up at the beam. We hear a car pull up outside, engine turns off. FLAN *peers out, nervous and unsure.*

FLAN. Is it the new daddy then? Is it? Haha! Joe boy! Congratulations! Congratulations!

JOE (*entering*). Christ, Flan. Yer well on it.

FLAN. Not so well that we can't share a drop o' this! (*Pulls out a little bottle of whiskey.*) To wet the babby's head an' all. Be rude not to.

He opens the bottle and passes it to JOE, *who takes a swig.*

What's he like? What's he like, Joe?

JOE. Looks just like his mam.

FLAN. Lucky fer him then, hah?

JOE. He's small but… they say he'll be fine.

FLAN. Didn't he give us all a fright, hah! Didn't he just.

JOE. She's sleepin' now.

FLAN. Christ aren't they a marvel. The women I mean. What they can do, hah? Give life, Joe boy. They give life, an' that's some skill. God must've seen we weren't up fer the job. Thank Christ. (*Swigs.*) What'll ya call him?

JOE (*thinks for a moment*). Jesus…

FLAN. Jesus?

JOE. No, ya feckin eejit.

FLAN. Well that's what you just said there.

JOE. I can't remember if we even agreed on a name.

FLAN. He'd get an awful hard time round these parts with a name / like Jesus.

JOE. There's a fog on my brain.

FLAN *passes him the bottle.*

Is it done?

FLAN. Pit's dug.

JOE. Good man.

FLAN. Shame though, awful waste've / good meat.

JOE. I just want rid of it.

FLAN *takes another swig. A bird shrieks outside. Dog starts barking.* FLAN *goes quickly to the door and peers out. Nothing. He sits again.*

Pause.

I've bin thinkin'…

FLAN. Don't be doin' too much've that now. Does no one any good does too much thinkin'.

JOE. Should we build a barricade?

FLAN. Hah?

JOE. To keep 'em out.

FLAN. What?

JOE. A barricade to keep 'em out. Folk up north've started doin'
it. Parts of England too. All the farms with the surplus
fodder. I think we should. To keep the bastards out. Whoever
they are. We need to keep 'em out.

Scene Thirteen

*Darkness. A baby cries. Lights up on farmhouse kitchen. It's
raining heavily outside. We hear* KITTY *soothing the child
upstairs somewhere. After a few moments,* JOE *enters, followed
by* FLAN. *They remove outdoor clothes.*

FLAN. Miserable out there.

JOE. It is.

FLAN. Dirty old night.

JOE. Sit down there an' I'll get us a drink.

FLAN. Fine set've lungs on him, hah?

JOE. He's a strong lad. Gettin' stronger every day.

FLAN. An' no name yet?

JOE. Not yet. Needs to be right. Needs to be the right one.

> JOE *goes off for the drinks.* FLAN *sits down. There's a pack
> of cards on the table. He starts dealing.* JOE *re-enters with
> two glasses of whiskey.*

FLAN. A wee game?

JOE. Go on then.

FLAN. All clear tonight so.

JOE. Tonight.

He picks up his cards. They start to play. JOE *lays down the first meld.*

FLAN. Everyone's talkin' 'bout it.

JOE. Let them talk.

FLAN. You've started a trend. Mick Dwyer's building one now.

JOE. Yeah?

FLAN. And his neighbour, Con Sullivan, he's doing the same. Had intruders too y'see. Barricades goin' up all over the shop. (*Pause.*) 'S from the French for barrel. Did you know that? '*Barrique.*' (*Pause.*) Normally it's Greek or Latin. Where they come from like. The words I mean.

JOE. Put a card down.

FLAN. Hah?

JOE. Put a card down. It's your turn.

FLAN. Is it?

JOE. Yeah.

FLAN draws one card from the stock pile, then puts down a meld of cards.

You can't do that.

FLAN. Hah?

JOE. You can't do that.

FLAN. Why not? Same suit.

JOE. The order's wrong. Yer missin' the four of hearts. See? Two of hearts, three of hearts, five of hearts. You can't just jump between three an' five like that.

FLAN. Ah.

JOE. Consecutive order.

FLAN. I know, I know. (*Changes the meld.*) There. (*Sits back and folds his arms. Pause.*) What?

JOE. Discard.

FLAN *discards*.

Face up.

FLAN. Christ's sake!

FLAN *adjusts card.* KITTY *enters quietly from upstairs.*

KITTY. Fast asleep.

FLAN. Yer a marvel, Kitty. He's a grand wee fella so he is.

KITTY. When he sleeps… the way he holds himself… same as you, Joe.

FLAN. Hang on, we playin' aces high or low?

JOE. Both.

FLAN. But I thought we was playin' them low?

JOE. Why? We always play them both ways.

FLAN. Ah fer feck's sake!

A noise comes from outside and the dog starts barking. JOE *moves immediately to the window, turning out the light and collecting the rifle on his way.*

It's just a fox runnin' through.

JOE. Shssssh! (*Hushed voice.*) There!

FLAN *moves to window.* KITTY *stays where she is.*

FLAN. Where?

JOE. There! See?

FLAN. Can't see nothin' 'cept rain, Joe boy.

JOE. I saw somethin'. I know I did.

FLAN. There's nothin' there, Joe.

JOE. There! (*Looks out as if he's just seen something move past the window.*).

KITTY. Can you see anything, Flan?

FLAN. We built a barricade, fer Christ's sake. There's nothin' out there. There's nothin' out there tonight.

JOE. I'd a dream about them.

KITTY. Why don't ya go up to him? You've not seen him all day.

FLAN. That's an idea, hah? Go on up there an' look in on yer new babby, Joe.

A beam from a flashlight outside crosses the window suddenly. It goes.

Pause.

Beam of light passes over room again. It goes.

Silence apart from rain.

The sudden sound of a large bird screeching.

Then the phone starts ringing. Nobody answers it. JOE *exits abruptly, taking the rifle with him, followed by* FLAN.

KITTY *is frozen on the spot, staring at the phone that continues to ring.*

Darkness.

Scene Fourteen

Light up on INTERVIEWER. *She's talking to someone we can't see.*

INTERVIEWER. Don't feel like it today? (*Pause*.) We all have days like that I suppose. (*Pause*.) I see a lot of people like you. People who just… (*Pause*.) Ever heard of the *hikikomori*? It's this trend in Japan. I read about it. Magazine in the doctor's waiting room. Had an appointment yesterday. Sleeping problems. Anyway these kids in Japan, they just… withdraw from everything. Cut themselves off. Some don't leave their room for years. The lost generation they call them. The *hikikomori*. A way of expressing their dissatisfaction with it all you see. With the system. Happening everywhere now. All over the world. People in their thirties, forties. Millions of them. Just… fed up to the hilt. And they want out. They've had enough and they want out. (*Pause*.) Millions of them.

Scene Fifteen

Lights up on interior of the hay shed. JOE *is sitting on a hay bale with the rifle. His eyes are deadpan, exhausted. He has injured his hand. Dog starts barking as footsteps approach the hay shed.* JOE *relaxes when he hears* KITTY*'s voice hushing the dog. She enters.*

JOE. Couldn't keep up. Too fast.

KITTY. Time to come in now.

JOE. Five've them. Maybe six. Flan saw them too. He saw them this time.

KITTY. I've left him with the baby. You'd swear I asked him to mind a ten-foot cobra.

JOE. They were laughin'.

KITTY. Time to come in.

JOE. The fields are full of water. It was like… moving through black sludge.

KITTY. Need to disinfect that.

JOE (*to himself*). Fuck them. Hope they burn in hell.

KITTY (*easing the rifle out of his hands*). Sleep. Rest.

JOE. Where'll we go?

KITTY. We're not goin' anywhere.

JOE. They're comin', Kitty.

KITTY. We're not goin' anywhere.

JOE. They'd motorbikes this time. Heard the engines start but… couldn't see nothin'. Couldn't see through the rain. They kept goin' round and round.

KITTY. Young fellas messin' / about just.

JOE. NO!

Silence. He looks at covered-up boat.

I've not finished it yet.

KITTY. No matter.

JOE. There's a flood coming.

KITTY. You need rest, Joe.

JOE (*studies her face for a moment*). Like Maureen O'Hara. (*Pause.*) You know I…

KITTY. I know.

Pause.

JOE. What about Lorcan? I was thinkin' Lorcan.

KITTY (*considers it*). Yeah. I like that.

JOE. Do ya?

KITTY. Yeah. It's nice.

JOE. Means 'little fierce one'.

KITTY. Let's go in.

JOE. Can we call him Lorcan?

KITTY. Sure there's no rush, we can think / on it some –

JOE. It's a good name, Kitty. A strong name. He needs a strong name!

KITTY. Alright. Alright. But let's go in first. Can we do that first?

They go to exit, KITTY *takes the rifle with her.* JOE *pauses at the door.*

JOE. Rain's stopped. Not seen that moon in a long time. (*Pause.*) It's spinning away you know.

KITTY. I know.

JOE *touches* KITTY*'s face gently. He kisses her.*

Think I hear him crying.

They exit.

Scene Sixteen

Lights up on FLAN *standing in the middle of the yard. It is very early morning and he has just come out of the hay shed. Light rain. His hands are trembling. He looks towards the house for a moment, then back towards the hay shed. A flock of birds swoop overhead and startle him. He looks up to the sky.*

FLAN (*whispering*). 'And I give eternal life to them, and they will never perish; and no one will snatch them out of My hand.'

He blesses himself, then pulls out a little flask of whiskey from his inside pocket and takes a swig. He looks towards the hay shed again.

Jesus, Joe.

*He takes another swig. The sound of a baby crying comes
from inside the house. He looks at the house for a long while.
Baby continues to cry. He takes one last swig then starts
walking slowly towards the house. Lights fade.*

Scene Seventeen

Day six. KITTY *is looking out the window.* INTERVIEWER
enters. She looks weary.

Her hair is loose around her shoulders.

KITTY. You're late.

INTERVIEWER. The floods are bad.

    INTERVIEWER *unpacks in silence, places the Dictaphone
on the table and presses record.*

    Day six… (*Realises she's forgotten her watch. Pause.*) Day
six.

KITTY. 'And the rain was on the earth for forty days and forty
nights.'

    Silence.

    Can I see Lorcan?

INTERVIEWER. That's not possible right now.

KITTY. Just want to say hello.

INTERVIEWER. They won't let you.

KITTY. Been two weeks now. They've no right.

INTERVIEWER. Yes they do.

KITTY. They've no right to / keep me from –

INTERVIEWER. They have every right because they're in
control, not you!

    Long pause.

I'm sorry. The floods last night, they… the place I'm… it's a mess. Three porcelain cups kept floating round like little boats.

KITTY. So why are you here?

INTERVIEWER. You think I have a choice? (*Pause. Laughs.*) Ginny wanted to lie down but she couldn't. She just kept splashing from room to room, looking for a dry spot all night long.

KITTY. Who's Ginny?

INTERVIEWER. My dog. I brought her with me. I always bring her with me.

Pause.

KITTY. That woman, she was only thirty.

INTERVIEWER. What woman.

KITTY. The one swept away in the car. I told you about her, remember? At least you weren't swept away. (*Pause.*) There's a flood coming. A big one.

Pause.

INTERVIEWER. Why?

KITTY. Why what?

INTERVIEWER. Why do you want to see him? Why do you want to see Lorcan?

KITTY. What kind've a question's that? You think I don't care about him? Is that it? Well if that's what you think then you can fuck off out the door right now. Go on, fuck off an' tell them to send someone else from hereon in!

INTERVIEWER. I'm / sorry.

KITTY. You can't just sit there an' judge me. What would you have done?

Pause.

INTERVIEWER. I'll see what I can do.

Silence.

KITTY. It's a mess isn't it. An awful mess. But we can't go back. (*Pause.*) You know, if the floods don't do it then the sun will. Already happening. The solar storms? Like the one back in '89? Knocked out every bulb in Canada. All those people without light. All squirming in the dark. (*Pause.*) The floods will do it though. I dreamt about it a long time ago. Listen. Can you hear? That water out there just keeps on rising.

INTERVIEWER *looks at her for a long moment, then starts making some notes.*

Scene Eighteen

Lights up on farmhouse kitchen. A body lies on the table covered with a sheet. FLAN is standing at the window looking out, a glass of whiskey in his hand. A door closes quietly from upstairs and KITTY enters. She goes and sits by the body. Silence apart from the sound of a mosquito buzzing round the room and KITTY's gentle humming. The mosquito buzzing stops. FLAN slaps his arm hard.

FLAN. Damn mosquitoes. Vicious little things. Been around fer millions of years y'know. Adapt y'see. From the Arctic to the equator. Outlast us all so they will. (*Pause.*) Should we... Should I not call someone now.

KITTY *keeps on humming.*

They need to... We should call them. When you're ready. Just... tell me when you're ready.

KITTY. He used like that song. His father too.

FLAN. Not in his right mind. Not thinkin' straight.

KITTY (*takes a note from her pocket and hands it to FLAN*). He was thinkin' straight alright.

FLAN *reads.*

Left it upstairs. In the baby's cot. He was tryin' to save the farm. For us. For me an' Lorcan. (*Laughs.*) But they won't be payin' out. They won't be payin' out, Joe.

KITTY *goes to a drawer and rummages through. She pulls out a document, opens it, finds a certain page then hands it to* FLAN.

Top've the page. I've marked it.

FLAN (*reads*). '...if the policy holder dies by suicide within four years from the policy issue date, then any beneficiaries will... will not be able to...'

KITTY. He was thinkin' straight, but not straight enough. Those bastards catch you every way they can. (*Pause.*) Help me.

FLAN. Of course I will. Of course I will, Kitty. Who d'you want me to call first?

KITTY. No. I mean... I want you to help me.

FLAN. What d'you mean?

KITTY. If they find out, then they'll take it off me. They'll take it all away. What's left of it. And Joe'll have... it'll all be fer nothin'. An' I won't let that happen. Enough. Enough now. D'you understand. Enough.

Lights fade. Darkness.

Scene Nineteen

O'Flaherty's Bar. Still no electricity.

INTERVIEWER. Didn't think you'd be open. It's nice that you are. A place to go. (*Drinks.*) Suppose I should be getting off.

BARMAN. One for the road?

INTERVIEWER. What road. There are no roads. (*Laughs.*) People are out there in boats! (*Pause.*) Sure if you couldn't laugh, you'd cry. I'm a bit drunk. What colour are your eyes?

BARMAN. Blue.

INTERVIEWER. They look grey to me. I was in love once. He had grey eyes.

Silence.

BARMAN. Hospital's flooded.

INTERVIEWER. Is it?

BARMAN. Yeah.

INTERVIEWER. They evacuate?

BARMAN. Most. Not all. Electricity's gone. There are rumours.

INTERVIEWER. What rumours.

BARMAN. Euthanasia.

INTERVIEWER. What?

BARMAN. To stop the pain.

INTERVIEWER. I don't...

BARMAN. Some won't last long enough for rescue.

INTERVIEWER. But they can't... they can't do that. That's murder.

BARMAN. Only saying what I've heard. Can you find the funny in that?

Silence. She drinks.

INTERVIEWER. Day six. Day six and nothing. Still fucking... nothing. (*Pause.*) I hate my job.

She drinks.

BARMAN. He said somethin' to me. Night before he left town.

INTERVIEWER. Who did?

BARMAN. Flan.

INTERVIEWER. The farmhand?

BARMAN. Aye. Flan. He said somethin' that stuck in my head. Drunk like, but... it stuck all the same.

INTERVIEWER. What did he say? (*Pause.*) What did he say.

Pause.

BARMAN. There's a field way out back with an oak tree. The old man used love that tree. Used joke about bein' buried underneath.

Pause.

INTERVIEWER. Is that it?

BARMAN *starts drying some glasses.*

BARMAN. They keep it closed off. Acorns can poison the cattle see, so it's in its own little enclosure. Quiet spot. Nice spot on a sunny day. They say it's been there for centuries, that tree. Last a long time them oaks do. Like a good granite headstone. A good granite headstone should keep a long time. (*Pause.*) 'Scuse me, I need to change a barrel.

BARMAN *exits. Pause. Then* INTERVIEWER *hurriedly exits.*

Scene Twenty

*Lights up on farmhouse kitchen. The body is gone. A radio is on
but the volume is down low. FLAN is standing looking at the
table where the body had previously lain.*

KITTY *enters in bathrobe, towel-drying her hair.*

KITTY. I told ya get out've those wet things. You'll catch yer
death. There's dry towels in there.

FLAN. They say more floods is comin'.

KITTY. Flan.

FLAN. All gone mad so it is.

KITTY. Go clean up.

FLAN. More floods means more mosquitoes. D'you remember
that man up north? Don't hear much about him no more.
Mosquito bite. Killed him stone dead. They're like an army.
An' we're their hosts. All this rain. All this damned rain.

KITTY. Go get out've those wet things.

FLAN. They found the Ark, Kitty. The Ark. On top of a
mountain somewhere in Turkey. Imagine that. 'The earth
was corrupt before God, so he will destroy them with the
earth.' (*Pause.*) What about that wee fella? You'll not
manage both. (*Pause.*) What we done is wrong. It's wrong so
it is. No priest to bless him, no consecrated / ground to…

KITTY. Stop it. An' don't you talk to me 'bout consecrated
ground. Don't you dare. Why's it only when we're dead folk
talk that way, when we're dead that folk care. What about the
living? (*Pause.*) Go get changed. We've the cows to bring in.

*A dog starts barking outside. She goes to window and looks
out.*

FLAN. This won't go away. (*Pause.*) An' they'll still want their
money.

The baby starts crying upstairs. Darkness.

Scene Twenty-One

Lights up on interview room. INTERVIEWER *is listening back to some of the tape.*

KITTY'S VOICE. He liked 'em see? Loved 'em. So that's where I'd... He was safer there. The house was too dangerous. Knives, sharp edges, stairs. I had no choice.

INTERVIEWER'S VOICE. So leaving him there was the best option?

KITTY'S VOICE. I had a farm to run. An' they'd bark. If there was someone out there. Someone that shouldn't be. The dogs would always let me know.

INTERVIEWER'S VOICE. He moves like one, Kitty.

Pause on recording.

Did you hear me? Your son moves like one. He thinks he's one of them.

Pause on recording.

Did you hear me? He *moves* like one 'cause he *thinks* / he's one.

KITTY'S VOICE. What did you want me to do? I had to take care of the farm. There was so much to... I couldn't let them... I couldn't let them win.

INTERVIEWER *stops the Dictaphone and contemplates for a moment. She replays the last part of the tape.*

What did you want me to do? I had to take care of the farm. There was so much to... I couldn't let them... I couldn't let them win.

She stops the tape and puts her head in her hands. KITTY *enters.*

KITTY. Thought we'd finished for the day.

INTERVIEWER. Sit down.

KITTY *sits.*

KITTY. I was going to wash my hair.

INTERVIEWER. Tell me about the tree. (*Pause.*) Tell me about the oak tree. (*Pause.*) You can see him if you tell me. I can have that arranged.

Scene Twenty-Two

The hay shed. KITTY *is stacking some feed sacks.* FLAN *is working alongside her in silence. A flood siren goes off in the distance.* FLAN *stops.*

KITTY. They're just testing the system.

FLAN goes back to work. They continue working in silence. The flood siren eventually stops.

FLAN. Can't go down O'Flaherty's no more. They all keep askin' questions. Folk's startin' to wonder. (*Pause.*) Been over a year now. They're startin' to think something's wrong up here. (*Pause.*) This isn't right.

KITTY. Don't you start up 'bout what's wrong an' what's right. My husband's corpse is rotting in the back field out there 'cause of what they've done. So don't you start up 'bout what's wrong an' what's right.

They both go back to work.

FLAN. He needs a bath. Filthy he is. Leavin' him there all day long like that.

KITTY. What d'you want me to do? Carry him round like a monkey on my back? I've a farm to run. He's safe there, you know that. The house is full of... there's the stairs for a start, an' those sharp edges round / the fireplace –

FLAN. Yesterday, yesterday I heard him make a sound like one. Like a dog, woman. A dog.

KITTY. He's safe there. It's a safe place. An' I'll give him his bath later.

Pause.

FLAN. 'Let the little children come to me, for the kingdom of God belongs / to such as these.'

KITTY. I'm not interested in what your God says or what anyone says, an' if ya don't like it, ya know what to do. I'm not / stoppin' ya.

FLAN. Should never've / done it.

KITTY. THEY'RE NOT TAKIN' THIS FARM OFF ME.

Silence.

FLAN. Johnny Donnelly, Rob Moriarty, Liam Kennedy. Ned Callaghan, Con Sullivan, Mick Dwyer. Mary O'Connor from the greengrocer's. Dominic Mulhall down the creamery. Jack O'Shea, Paddy O'Shea, Brian Loughlin. Sean Leahy, Thomas Murphy and what's-his-name, that vet's assistant fella, Eoin Robinson. Dermot McCarthy, Gillian Sweeney, Michael Walsh. Bill and Deirdre Fitzpatrick. Roger Fitzgerald. Dan O'Leary, Mairead Reagan, Jonathan Lyons, Dave McKenna, Frances Wycherley, Kyle Wycherley, all of 'em. All of 'em an' more. Askin' questions, Kitty. They keep on askin' an' askin' an' I can't stand it no more!

Silence. Rain starts to fall.

My mind's made up.

FLAN *goes to door.*

KITTY. Don't tell them, Flan. Please. Don't tell them. (*Pause.*) I just want to be left alone. I just want them to leave us alone now.

Pause.

FLAN. I'll not be back.

He exits. KITTY *stands there for a while, unsure of what to do next. She looks to the beam. Then she walks to the half-finished boat, uncovers it, picks up a hammer and starts hammering.*

Scene Twenty-Three

INTERVIEWER *is waiting. She's continuing to play back parts of the tape*

KITTY'S VOICE. The day starts.

Breath.

Bring the cows up for feeding.

Separate the sick ones.

Call the vet maybe.

Take the cows back to the field.

Hose down the feeding shed.

Check fencing.

Check machinery.

Do planning and purchasing.

Spray for weeds.

Check the records.

Sort out the schedules.

Bring them up for second feed.

Breath.

Hose it down again.

Take them back to the field.

Keep them in if the fields are bad.

Watch for calving cows.

Assist as needed.

Office again.

More paperwork.

More planning.

More purchasing.

Check the drainage.

Do shed maintenance.

Clean the yard.

Breath.

Haymaking should be underway.

'Cept it's not 'cause of all this fucking rain.

All this awful rain.

Check the sick ones again.

Remember to feed the dogs.

Don't forget to feed the dogs.

Try to sleep.

Try to get some sleep.

But someone's still watching.

Next day an' it all starts over again.

It all starts all over again.

Breath. Then pause on recording.

Christ's sake! I was on my own out there. What did you want me to do?

Pause of recording.

I tried to keep him safe.

KITTY *enters and* INTERVIEWER *switches off Dictaphone. Long pause.*

KITTY. You've cut his hair. He looks like his father. They wouldn't let me stay long. An' I couldn't hold him. He has lots of nice things. Nice toys. (*Pause.*) I would've liked to have held him.

INTERVIEWER. They can't just… We can't just leave him there.

KITTY. 'S where his daddy wanted to be buried.

INTERVIEWER. There's nothing registered. There's no certificate.

KITTY. What difference does any of that make now. (*Pause.*) They'll think I did it won't they? Well it wasn't me who killed him. It wasn't me who / did that.

INTERVIEWER. I know, I believe / you.

KITTY. It wasn't me who did that. (*Pause.*) Couldn't let them find out. They'd have taken it all away. That was our farm. Our home. We'd worked so hard.

INTERVIEWER. I'm sorry.

KITTY. It's not your fault. At least I don't think it is. I don't know whose fault it is. Do you?

Silence.

A heavy shower starts. Almost deafening. It subsides after a few moments.

INTERVIEWER. Damn rain.

KITTY. Can you smell that? There's something in the air. Like… earth. The smell of earth. Like something's stirring. (*Pause.*) Was it six? Or was it seven?

INTERVIEWER. Sorry?

KITTY. Number of days it took him. To create it all. Six wasn't it? An' he rested on the seventh. Right?

INTERVIEWER. I think so. Though I'm not the best person to be asking.

KITTY. Don't know if I believe any more either. (*Pause.*) I'm not a bad person.

INTERVIEWER. I don't think you are.

KITTY. I was just… I was just trying to… What would you have done?

Long pause. KITTY *smiles, then stands and goes to the window.*

Once, when Lorcan was very small, a few weeks or so, I was stood by the bedroom window. Had him in my arms. Could see Joe in the back field with the dogs driving the cows up. Flan was with him. They were laughin' 'bout something. It was good to see him laugh. I'd not seen him laugh fer a long time. I stood there an' watched 'em come up through the field. The rain had stopped an' the sun was out an' it all felt good for a moment. (*Pause.*) Then I saw it. Standin' by the hedge out in the distance. Shadowy thing. Watchin' them, just like I was. Stood there watchin' them. (*Pause.*) And after a while, it turned its head an' looked at me. Looked straight at me. (*Pause.*) Flan an' Joe were still laughin' but the baby started cryin'. An' the phone started ringing downstairs. An' then it was gone. (*Pause.*) I never told Joe. I never did. I… I just wiped it away. Like you wipe chalk off a blackboard. (*Pause.*) All we needed was some time.

Heavy shower outside again.

Maybe Flan was right. Maybe he really is going to reset the world. Maybe that's the only way to put it all right.

Silence.

Then the flood siren goes off.

They look at each other for a moment.

Lights start flickering on and off.

Sudden darkness.

End of play.